the MESSAGE of the Bible

MARTYN LLOYD-JONES

the woman] shall bruise thy [the serpent's] head" (Genesis 3:15). The serpent can only be mastered by one, and he has come—the seed of the woman, Jesus of Nazareth.

"

> *For God so loved the world, that he gave his only begotten Son, that whosoever believeth in him should not perish, but have everlasting life.*
>
> JOHN 3:16

Christ, the Son of God, came into this world, took on our human nature, entered into our very situation, and defeated our enemy. He received judgment for us on the cross. God dealt with him there and pardons us, and our enemy is conquered. So the way to paradise is open, and it is open for you.

All your problems, all your needs, arise from the fact of sin. That is the cause of all ill. And there

Man, as the result of all this, is quite helpless; he has brought a curse upon himself and cannot escape it. He would like to, but he cannot. Man has been trying to get back into Eden ever since he went out of it. That is the whole history of civilization. That is the whole meaning of philosophy and all political thought and all the blueprints of utopias at all times and in all places— man trying to get back into paradise.

But it is worse than merely not being in paradise. Man is under the judgment of God. He thought that he could forget God and that there would be no risk involved. He did not realize that the law of God is absolute. Both man as an individual and the whole world, according to the Bible, are under the judgment of God. You see, in the garden Adam and Eve thought they could eat the forbidden fruit and all would be well. Then they heard the voice of the Lord God, and they cowered and were frightened. Judgment had come, and they were thrust out.

But, thank God, he intervenes! God, even at the moment of rebellion, tells man that he has a way to rescue him and to redeem him: "It [the seed of

We are all aware of problems in this world. Everyone knows what it is to be weary, to be disappointed, and to struggle. And we have a feeling that we were not meant for this. We are all searching for some solution to the problems of life.

The question is, why are you unhappy? Why do things go wrong? Why is there illness and sickness? Why should there be death? Those are the questions with which the Bible deals.

The Bible talks to you about your unhappiness. Some insist that the Bible, far from being practical, is really very remote from life. But nothing in the world is as practical as the teaching of the Bible.

In order to answer questions about you, the Bible starts in the most extraordinary way:

"

In the beginning God . . .

It starts with God. Before I begin to ask any questions about myself and my problems, I ought to ask questions like this: Where did the world come from? Where have I come from? What is life itself?

You come to me and say, "I'm unhappy. I'm in a crisis. What's the matter with me?" And the Bible says, "In the beginning God . . ." as if it has forgotten all about you. But it has not! The only way to understand yourself or your life is to start with God. And right at the very beginning, the Bible takes us there.

The Bible also tells us that the world came into being because the eternal God made it. It tells us that God is the Creator, that he made everything out of nothing, by his own power, and he made it perfect.

What's more, according to the Bible, man is a special creation of God. The Bible tells us, "God created man in his own image" (Genesis 1:27). It does not say that about anything else, only about human beings. Man was made by God, for God. He spoke to God, walked with God, and enjoyed God. And his life was one of perfect bliss.

But into this perfect world made by God there entered another power, another force. Something came that was opposed to God and opposed to man, and it was bent upon one thing only—wrecking God's perfect work. The Bible tells us that the Devil entered into this world, and by tempting the man and the woman, whom God had made, brought to pass everything bad that you and I know.

Why are there jealousy and envy and misunderstanding? Why lust and passion? Why are homes and marriages broken? Why do little children suffer? Why all the agony and the pain of life?

It is because there is this other power in the world that has dragged man down. That is the biblical explanation. You will find it in the Bible from beginning to end. And if that is true, how hopelessly and utterly inadequate are all the remedies that are being offered apart from the Bible. What's more, the Bible tells us that as the result of that original sin, all of us are in the grip of this evil power.

is but one solution to the problem, the solution that God himself has provided in the person of his Son. ". . . that whosoever believeth in him should not perish, but have everlasting life." And that life begins here and now—a knowledge of God, assurance that you are right with God, that he will take you through death and announce in the judgment that you are already pardoned and forgiven.

My dear friend, that is your problem, and that is the answer to your problem. Believe it. Accept it here and now. Go to that great God. Acknowledge your sinning against him, and thank him for his eternal love in sending his Son to rescue you and to redeem you by dying for you, and ask him to give you new life. And he will. I say that on the authority of Jesus who stated, "Him that cometh to me I will in no wise cast out" (John 6:37).

Adapted from *The Gospel in Genesis: From Fig Leaves to Faith* written by Martyn Lloyd-Jones. Published by Crossway, © 2009.

MARTYN LLOYD-JONES (1899-1981)

*The minister of Westminster Chapel
in London for 30 years, he was one
of the foremost preachers of his
day. His many books have brought
profound spiritual encouragement
to millions around the world.*

CROSSWAY

GOOD
NEWS
Tracts

ISBN 978-1-6821-6380-1

9 781682 163801

www.goodnewstracts.org